With love to our little angel, Zach
~ Mimi

# THE WISE ANIMAL HANDBOOK

Kate B. Jerome

ARCADIA KIDS

Attempt new **skills** from **time** to **time.**

Just **try** to think them **through.**

# And if you find you're left behind...

...then change your point of view.

# Try not to think of just yourself.

Invent new ways to share.

Stay **close** to friends whom you can trust.

But
always
be
aware.

# Avoid
the
## tattle
in the
## tale.

Insist that **truth** is **best.**

# Embrace with pride the strengths you have.

Demand
to be
impressed.

# Enjoy
the
# peace
that
# nature
brings.

Ignore what's just for show.

# Join forces when the road gets rough.

Admit
when you
don't know.

Remember **family** is the **best.**

Despite the **ups** and **downs.**

# Don't **hide** from things that you must **face.**

Make
joyful
laughing
sounds.

Eat healthy food to grow up strong.

Be **patient** with your **friends.**

# Try not to take a stubborn stand.

Be quick to make amends.

# Excuse yourself when manners slip.

Be helpful every day.

# Keep **trying** even when it's **hard.**

But don't forget to play!

And

sing

...and **dance** each **day!**

Written by Kate B. Jerome
Design and Production: Lumina Datamatics, Inc.
Coloring Illustrations: Tom Pounders
Research: Eric Nyquist

Cover Images: See back cover

Interior Images: 002 Anetapics/Shutterstock.com; 003 George Green/Shutterstock.com; 004 Sergey
Uryadnikov/Shutterstock.com; 005 Gnomeandi/Shutterstock.com; 006 Bruce MacQueen/Shutterstock.com;
007 Henk Bentlage/Shutterstock.com; 008 M.M./Shutterstock.com; 009 Mikael Damkier/Shutterstock.com; 010
Brendan van Son/Shutterstock.com; 011 Michael Pettigrew/Shutterstock.com; 012 StevenRussellSmithPhotos/
Shutterstock.com; 013 Pakhnyushchy/Shutterstock.com; 014 Patjo/Shutterstock.com; 015 Quinn Martin/
Shutterstock.com; 016 Lincoln Rogers/Shutterstock.com; 017 Dirk Ercken/Shutterstock.com; 018 Karel Gallas/
Shutterstock.com; 019 Orangecrush/Shutterstock.com; 020 Guenter-foto/Shutterstock.com; 021 Janecat/
Shutterstock.com; 022 Shironina/Shutterstock.com; 023 Annette Shaff/Shutterstock.com; 024 Vitaly
Titov/Shutterstock.com; 025 Rohappy/Shutterstock.com; 026 MattiaATH/Shutterstock.com; 027 Otsphoto/
Shutterstock.com; 028 FikMik/Shutterstock.com; 029 Four Oaks/Shutterstock.com; 030 Ekaterina Kolomeets/
Shutterstock.com; 031 Hugh Lansdown/Shutterstock.com.

Published by Arcadia Kids, a division of Arcadia Publishing and
The History Press, Charleston, SC

For all general information contact Arcadia Publishing at:
Telephone: 843-853-2070
Email: sales@arcadiapublishing.com

For Customer Service and Orders:
Toll Free: 1-888-313-2665
Visit us on the Internet at www.arcadiapublishing.com

Library of Congress Cataloging-in-Publication data is on file with the publisher.

Printed in China